A Guide
For
Everyday Living

A Guide
For
Everyday Living

A manual to help people with
disabilities function in everyday life

Stephen Landry

To order additional copies of this book, contact:
Xlibris Corporation
1-888-795-4274
www.Xlibris.com
Orders@Xlibris.com
53615

CONTENTS

Special Thanks

I would like to thank my family for helping me develop these systems and become a more confident and independent person:

Thelma J. Tibbitts, my mother, for being there every step of the way;

Catherine M. Langtry, my sister, for helping through difficult times;

Brian J. Landry, my brother, for repairing everything ASAP when called upon;

Karin J. Landry, my sister, for using her knowledgeable resources within the healthcare field to get me case management services to meet my needs;

and Stephen C. Landry Jr., my son, for being the inspiration for everything I've done.

I'd also like to thank Dr. Conrad Mark and his office manager, Maureen McDevitt, for the help they've given me over the years.

Last but not least, a special thanks to Judi Weston (cousin) and Christine Kelly (sister) for typing and editing this book. They helped me get my message out in my own words.

INTRODUCTION

After surgery in September of 1988, I was left with permanent, short-term memory impairment. I am writing this book to explain some systems I have developed by myself, and with the help of my family, to cope with this disability.

I had to redesign the way I lived and performed such everyday tasks as running a household and running errands. Re-training myself took time and practice and at first resulted in frustration and anger from dealing with the impairment I must now live with daily. Every day, out in society and the hustle and bustle of life, people do not have or wish to make time to cope with an individual with a disability.

A Word About Responsibility

Reaching the point of going through rehabilitation and/or recovery requires you to take responsibility for your actions. For example, when you run an errand, you are taking on the responsibility of making sure you complete it. *Do not bite off more than you can chew!* Do not become a "yes" man or woman just because situations may flow in a more positive manner. Take on only what is in your ability to complete successfully. At the same time, do not shy away from a task or situation that is a little bit of a challenge. Taking on some small challenges will help you grow beyond your disability.

When people with disabilities try to re-enter society, be it after rehabilitation from an accident or after a surgery, it can seem as if they are walking against an oncoming tide. I hope this book will provide you with little life preservers along your way.

The purpose of this book is to enable people to be self-sufficient in life while performing everyday tasks such as food shopping, running errands, housekeeping, paying bills and other daily and monthly activities.

About The Author

I am 51 and have had to deal with a head injury since the age of 2. In 1988, I also had corrective surgery for a seizure disorder which has left me with permanent short-term memory impairment. This was a big change in my life. At various times I would think, "Will this ever get any better?", better enough to take control of my life, to enable me to function within my daily life? It has gotten better through strong family support and much self determination. I hope these tools help you as much as they've helped me.

"A pen and my paper are my only prosthesis." Stephen Landry

A Note from the Author

These are proven systems created by me and my family following my brain surgery. With the help of rehabilitation and family support, I have learned needed strategies which allow me to function independently in life on a daily basis. These systems were developed from a strong need to control my own life and destiny rather than letting the "system" take care of it for me. Some of my successes include:

1   I work two jobs for a total of 12 hours per day
2   I own my own home
3   I have raised a strong and loving son

I list these accomplishments to show you that if you are a person with a disability, it does not mean the world has ended. Having a disability just means you have to go about things in life with a different approach than those who do not have a disability. These tools will help.

Remember just because you are brain injured it DOES NOT!! mean that you are brain dead. It just means that you have to go about things in life in a much more detailed way than others do when completing tasks or going places. Using this kind of system really will make you a much more efficient person and you will be able to complete tasks successfully.

To paraphrase John F. Kennedy:

> *"Don't ask what other people can do for you, ask what you can do for yourself in order to conquer the madness of everyday living."*

1. DAILY ACTIVITIES

*"Don't let society conquer you with their meaningless motion systems.
Find which system is best for you and your needs and run with it."*

One of the biggest challenges to any head injured person is to organize your daily activities to restore order and calm to a chaotic life. Some of the tools presented here will help reduce the confusion and frustration as you go through activities that most people take for granted. These tools have been proven by the author to be useful and easy to use after an initial set-up period. Family members or friends can assist with setting up these tools and helping make them routne.

Using a Day-Timer®

Managing daily activities requires a process for alerting you to what needs to be done and notifying you of what has already been done. I have a Day-Timer® notebook system that has proven to be my most useful tool to function successfully in daily life. For instance, the Day-Timer® helps me organize my activities and appointments and helps me keep track of the money I have in my wallet. All Day-Timers® can be purchased with sections for daily, weekly or monthly schedules, address books, budget pages, notes and shopping lists. Day-Timer® can be purchased at any office supply store such as Staples or Office Deport. Once purchased, the company will send you reminders when it is time to place your next order. Day-Timers® can also be purchased from:

DayTimers Inc.
One DayTimer Plaza
Allentown, PA 18195-1551

The Day-Timer® notebook system has proven to be my best prosthesis. This is not only because of the book itself, but also because it gives you so many different options for setting up your daily, weekly and monthly tasks. The first step to using this system is to set it up to meet your needs.

Setting up Daily Activities
(on your calendar or within your Day-Timer®)

The best way to accomplish things on a daily basis is to know what has to be done. To do this, get into the habit of recording your activities on a calendar or within a Day-Timer®. This will allow you to know when and where you have to be.

To set up your day to be most helpful, list each activity by date, time, location and with whom the activity will happen. For example, an entry might say: 7/30/09, 9:45AM, Jiffy Lube, Burlington. This gives you all the information you need about that appointment—date, time and location. This way, you will be able to schedule other activities throughout the day, or know that you have time to run another errand at 10:30 or 11:00.

Because each entry requires enough information to allow its completion, the tool that you choose must have enough space on which to write. Something that has one page per day will make it easier and clearer to record activities. (See sample page in Tool section).

Tracking Money in Your Wallet

Another good use for your daily activity tool is to help you keep track of your money. Often, unless you write it down, you may find yourself at the end of the day wondering where all of your money went. I have had a lot of success using my Day-Timer® for this purpose.

To start my money tracking, I initial the bottom of the page everyday with "BB." This stands for "Beginning Balance." Next, I count the money in my wallet and record the total next to "BB." For example, "BB" = $40.00. This tells me how much money I have when I start my day. During the day, as I spend money, I record how much I spent and what I bought. For example, "$10.00—Gas." I continue this throughout the day and total what I have spent at the end of the day. I record the total next to the initials "DT" (Daily Total). Once done, I subtract what I spent from my beginning balance (BB) to get how much money I should have in my pocket at the start of the day tomorrow. An example of the items I record in my Day-Timer® is shown below:

1.	$10.00 Gas	$40.00 BB
2.	$18.00 Food shopping	- $28.00 DT
3.	$28.00 DT	$12.00 left at the end of the day

Start the process over again the next day. In the example above, I'd write, "BB" = $12.00, for the next day. After awhile this will become a good habit that will help you keep control of where your money goes.

Even With a List

Even with a list, things such as errands could become complicated to do because people who wrote the list would not record enough information for me to perform the errand.

Two examples of typical errands might be to go to the Post Office and mail the bills, or go to the store to pick up milk. While both examples are simple tasks to perform, what often happens is that the person requesting the errand would say, "Oh, by the way, when you're at the Post Office, please pick me up a book of stamps."

Although, this can seem like part of the same errand (going to the Post Office), it too has to be written down to be successfully completed. Writing it down will eliminate forgetting and/or guessing other parts of your errand.

You may want to be prepared to prompt the other person if they need anything else so you can eliminate frustration and duplicate trips. (Note: Note pages to record this kind of information are available with the Day-Timer® system).

Notes can be taken with me so that I don't have to bring my whole book. That way I won't forget the book when I'm doing an errand. When the errand is complete, I check it off in my book and discard the note.

Telephone Numbers and Contacts

You should always have the telephone numbers of doctors, pharmacies, family and friends on hand so you do not have to look them up in a phonebook or call information when you need them.

Having this information available can be helpful at home, at work or in an emergency, and you will not have any added expense from directory assistance. This is where something such as the Day-Timer® system can be helpful. You may also want to find an alternative place for storing this type of information. When you set up your Day-Timer® or other tool, be sure to record this information in its appropriate place.

2. DRIVING

Driving can be a real hassle. Remembering landmarks or counting traffic lights can help you find your way back home. Using a GPS system or On-Star® can also be helpful for finding your way to and from work or home. Both GPS and On-Star® offer detailed instructions.

A good GPS system should be easy to use and give you spoken directions. You don't need to complicate driving by having to read directions on a screen. A Tom Tom or Magellan GPS works quite well and can be found in many electronic stores.

On-Star® now comes with many new cars. You will have to activate this system with the On-Star® company and there may be a monthly fee, but the system provides good, clear driving directions.

Parking the Car and Locating it Again

Parking the car should not be a difficult task, but for some of us it is. If you have a problem remembering where you parked while doing errands, here are some ideas that can help.

When you are out running errands, you cannot always find a parking spot right in front of your destination. What I tend to do in that situation is to park facing the main entrance of the store or building I am going into. In addition, I try to park against stationary fixtures such as an embankment, a light post or a fence.

Do not park beside a large or different type of car thinking it will be easy to remember, because chances are, when you return, it will be gone and will not provide a reminder.

If your car is equipped with keyless entry, you may be able to use the beep from the car or its' flashing lights when you press the button to help locate your vehicle.

Keys

What I am writing about now is something I call 'key adjustments'. What a key adjustment means is putting the keys on your key ring in the order that you use them the most to the least. This easy technique will help avoid fumbling with your keys when trying to enter your house, apartment or car, especially in foul weather.

Put your house or apartment key first. You will need to use this key to lock your residence before going to your car.

Next, put your car key second. This will allow you to quickly find each key when going from the house to the car. Having your keys organized and in your hand will allow you quick entry and keep you from getting soaked from rain or snow or from freezing in the cold.

3. RECEIVING, OPENING AND STORING MAIL

When receiving mail into the house from the mailbox, most people will glance at it and throw it on the counter to deal with later. This is not an efficient way of doing things. The mail is what keeps us and our households operating smoothly. Therefore, it should be gathered and kept in a specific place to look over as the day allows. I personally have an in-house mailbox that I look over everyday for advertisements, bills, etc. After reviewing the mail, I throw away all of the junk mail and put all the bills together with a rubber band to store for paying later.

4. MANAGING MONEY AND BANKING

Banking

The one place your want to be the least confused or uncertain about is with the bank. When in the bank, you are there to deal with your money in one way or another; deposits, withdrawals, checking or savings accounts.

You have to be accurate with the amount of money, date and account numbers when filling out a deposit or withdrawal slip for your checking or savings account. You have to list all of your checks and cash and correctly total the amount being deposited, while correctly deducting the amount of money you are getting back. All of this calculation must be done accurately in what can prove to be a stressful environment in a busy bank.

I like to figure out the calculations at home on a calculator before going to the bank so when I get there I know exactly how to fill out the forms. Another alternative is to bring extra copies of deposit and withdrawal slips home with you so you can fill them out when you make your calculations.

Note: It is best to use a deposit slip from your checkbook because your account number is located at the bottom of the deposit slip. However, if this is not possible, you can carry the account number in your wallet or purse and use a deposit or withdrawal slip that the bank provides. If you do not remember your number or carry a copy with you, don't panic. The bank teller can easily look it up for you.

In the Appendix section of this book you will find examples of properly filled out deposit and withdrawal slips. The forms at your bank may be slightly different so be sure to compare the two.

Budgeting

Budgeting money is important because it may be difficult to remember what bills and expenses will be due throughout the month. When you budget, you create a source of funds that allows you to pay these bills without wondering where the money will come from. Careful budgeting will also help prevent you from missing due dates for bills.

Before you can budget your money, you must first determine how much money you need on a monthly basis to meet your basic expenses. Then you need to calculate a weekly amount to save. The calculation should relate to how frequently you get paid. For example, if you only get paid twice a month, you would want to calculate your savings from two paychecks.

The first step is to gather all of your monthly bills. Be sure to include your rent or mortgage, credit card bills, car payment and utility bills. Be sure to include all bills on which you make a monthly payment.

Add the amount for all the bills together to get a monthly total. Divide this total by 4 if you are paid weekly and by 2 if you are paid bi-monthly. This is the amount you will have to deposit into your checking account from your paycheck each time you get paid.

The following example shows you how this can work:

Bills

Rent	$300.00
Telephone	$ 50.00
Electric	$ 50.00
Car Payment	$100.00
TOTAL	$500.00

For Weekly Pay Periods:

Total Bills	$500.00
Divided by # of	÷ 4
paychecks (4)	$125.00 per pay period

For Bi-monthly Pay Periods:

Total Bills	$500.00
Divided by # of	÷ 2
paychecks (2)	$250.00 per pay period

Paying Bills

Not until years after my surgery did I even attempt to pay a bill due to the uncertainty of financial matters. I didn't really know how to go about taking care of my financial needs as someone else had always done my bookkeeping for me. Finally, the time had come when I not only had to do this for myself, but I wanted to take control of my own finances. Before I developed my current system of paying bills, I would pay them, for example, on the third week of the month one time, and the fourth week of the month the next time. Pretty soon this way of paying bills allowed some of them to overlap, but some of them wound up being paid late. Late payments are not a good way to establish or keep your credit rating good! Therefore, a system had to be established for paying bills consistently and on time that would take my disability into account. I sat down with my sister and asked her how I could overcome this. Between the two of us we came up with a system that is the nearest we could come to foolproof.

In order to use this system, you must first create a checklist of all your monthly bills. Your checklist will have four columns: Bill Name, Amount Due, Date Paid and Check Number. You have one list for each month. Since most of the bills will be the same each month, you can create the list and make copies to use again and again. Below is an example of how the checklist might look. I would suggest keeping the list in a folder or notebook for easy reference. You can also find a blank checklist in the "Tools" section of this book.

Pay all bills at the same time to avoid an overlap or a late payment. List bills by priority such as:

1. Rent/mortgage
2. Electric
3. Oil/gas
4. Telephone
5. Insurance—car/house
6. Car payment
7. Credit cards

Extra spaces on the bill page should be used for bills that do not come in on a monthly basis such as excise tax for your car or the automobile repair you may have had to pay for that month.

This will enable you to keep track of all your expenses within the month.

To pay your bills, use the following steps:

a) Open envelope
b) Take out all advertisements and throw them away. These are just ways to make you spend more money.
c) Go to the page in your workbook that lists the correct bill for that month (for example, telephone).
d) Fill in the amount due, the date you paid it and the check number used so you can have a quick reference without having to look in many places to find a record of the payment.

On your checklist for the month, look for the bill you need to pay (see example, Electric). Record the amount due, the date the bill was paid and the check number. Continue in this manner until all your bills for the present month are paid.

When you have finished, you will know that you have received and paid all of the bills you were expecting and you have a single spot where all of your payment information is recorded.

Month: November Year: 2009			
Bill Name	Amount Due	Date Paid	Check #
Electric	38.52	11/22/09	122
Telephone	35.50	11/22/09	123

Blank spaces are for out-of-the ordinary monthly bills you may have such as car repairs or home maintenance.

Storing Records

To safely keep and store important banking and household records purchase either a file box or a 2-drawer file cabinet (I prefer the 2-draw file). Keep your records in a central location.

Purchase a box of hanging file folders and a box of clear view tabs with inserts. These items are easily found at Staples or Office Max or any other store that carries basic office supplies (such as Wal-Mart).

Label the tabs for each file. For example, banking deposits, receipts, statements, food shopping lists, budget envelopes, etc. works well. Use as many files as you need in order for you to easily locate at any given time the records that you need.

A Word about Debit Cards

A Debit Card is a very convenient way to make a withdrawal from your checking account without worrying about the hours of the bank. It's so easy it becomes a habit—one which you **cannot** afford. Not only do you have to be aware of when you withdraw money but you also have to subtract the transaction in your check book.

If you do not subtract debit card purchases/withdrawals, you will throw off your account balance which will then not be correct. Because the balance is not correct, all of your other transactions will be added or subtracted incorrectly and throw you further off track.

Some banks will offer overdraft protection. This means that if you mistakenly write a check without having enough money, you will be charged an insufficient funds fee. This can be as much as $25.00 per check.

This means that when you make a deposit, the bank will automatically take those fees right from your account. For example, you deposit $200 and record it in your check book but the bank takes $25.00 in fees, your account now has $175 not the $200 you thought it had. Without keeping careful track of your spending from your account, you could get far off track and have to call the bank to get your true balance.

Having a debit card may not be worth the trouble that can occur because of the ease of making a mistake.

5. SHOPPING AND PREPARING FOOD

Food Shopping

I myself have never had to do much food shopping other than to push the carriage down the aisles for someone else. As a result I never paid too much attention to it. However, I now have to and I found it very difficult because I did not know what to buy or where items were located in the store. For that reason I also had to create a system for getting my food.

It is easier and more efficient to go to the same store each week until you become familiar with the store. This will allow you to become more confident when you shop. Make your list aisle by aisle, beginning with number one and only write down the items you regularly use. This will eliminate you going down the same aisle twice and forgetting items. Write down the headings of the aisle and then the items needed in that aisle like this:

Aisle	*Item*
1) Produce:	grapes, oranges
2) Dairy:	milk
3) Cereal:	cornflakes

When you are preparing to go shopping, go through your cabinets and circle those items on your list that you need in each aisle.

When I pick the item from the shelf and place it in the carriage, I put a check inside the circle that indicates that I have what I need. I continue from aisle to aisle until I have completed finding the items I have circled.

I then go to the check out. Remember: you have only budgeted a certain amount of money for food shopping each week. If you have only budgeted $60.00, then you can only spend $60.00, otherwise you will be taking money from another part of your budget which will create a shortage elsewhere. You don't need this to happen!

If you have only budgeted $60.00 and your items ring up at $65.00 you will be faced with the embarrassing situation of having to decide which items to leave behind at the register. Using a small hand-held calculator can also help you keep track of what you are spending as you go along.

Don't worry about being self-conscious about having a list. I have found that people compliment me on my organization and want to know where they can get one. Wives want my system for their husbands.

Now that you have done your food shopping successfully using your list and it's headings, expand even more and become more self-sufficient by going to different stores with just a handwritten list of the items you need. You can write it in the same format as your printed list using headings such as Dairy: milk, cream, eggs, etc.

Your ability to perform this task successfully without being limited to just one store will allow you to pick up various items on sale that other stores may not offer. Many stores also do not keep the same hours of operation so this will allow you to better schedule your time for other errands or for personal time. You will no longer be limited to just one store.

Cooking

Everyone likes to eat, but not everyone knows how to cook!! I am one of those who don't know how. In addition, with my memory deficit, I have to have a simplistic way of preparing food. To follow a recipe, I have to have the ingredients written in a specific format with exact instructions and measurement, even for a recipe as simple as a stir-fry dish. For example, I would follow a recipe card that might read:

a)   cut up meat into small or medium pieces
b)   set temperature on stove to medium
c)   add and melt margarine or butter
d)   add meat, poultry and brown
e)   then add vegetables (fresh or frozen)
f)   cook until meat is done.

Write simplistic recipes, searching for easy things to cook.

6. HOLIDAYS AND GIFT BUYING

Beware! Shopping for gifts for holidays or birthdays is best when you have a specific item in mind and price range that will allow you to stay within your budget. Knowing what you want and how much you will spend will also help you to determine where to buy it and keep you from running all over town.

Following this process beforehand can save you from what I call "EMOTIONAL SPENDING." This kind of spending is what you do when you go into a store and have only $40.00 to spend. But this "other" gift has caught your eye and it's 60% off. But even with the 60% off it's not in your price range. This takes discipline. Don't "reason" with yourself. Stay strong and only purchase what you can afford or this will ruin your entire budgeting process and cause a lapse in payment of regular monthly bills.

Christmas Beware! The Christmas holiday can cause you to lose a month by getting caught up in the holidays from 11/26-12/25—Christmas! During this time period, life itself can become very chaotic! Bills keep coming in, banking and errands need to get done and dinners need to be prepared, etc., in addition to the holiday.

You have to stay collected and focused on one day at a time in order to complete each and every item successfully. The holiday season can disrupt your routine at any given time. Some strategies for staying focused are making lists for:

1. Tasks (around the house)
2. Errands (Shopping, dropping items off at the Post Office, etc.)

Remember to allow extra time for errands during the holiday season due to more travel congestion because everyone is out doing the same thing. You must do this to successfully complete your task or errands.

7. CLEANING

Cleaning the House/Apartment

The key to successfully cleaning is choosing the correct product designed to do the cleaning job you want to accomplish. For example, dish detergent is to loosen film of food from dishes just as furniture polish lifts dust and polishes your furniture. You have to determine what results you are looking for in a product and know whether or not that is mildew or hard water stains in your bathroom.

Reading the labels will help you know which products are the right ones for your jobs. Once you know which products work the best for you, add them to your shopping list so you will remember to check if you need them each time you go shopping. Keep track of when you need them just like you do with your groceries.

Laundry

To minimize confusion about what has been washed and what hasn't, have just one clothes hamper in a central location (usually the bathroom). When the hamper is full, wash the clothes. This will allow you to keep laundry to a minimum and you will not be overburdened with trying to figure out what is clean and what is not.

The following steps will help make laundry easier:

1. Empty the hamper
2. Sort clothes by color—lights, darks, whites, reds—always wash red items separately (or you may end up with pink clothes!)

3. Set the washer for the correct size of the load—large, medium, small
4. Set the water temperature for the color—when in doubt, cold works best
5. Add laundry detergent while the washer is filling with water
6. Add clothes to washer
7. When the washer stops, move clothes to the dryer
8. Check the lint tray and remove any lint
9. Set timer and start dryer
10. When dryer stops and clothes are dry, remove from dryer and fold
11. Place clean clothes in bureau, closet, etc.
12. Continue with remaining loads until all wash is complete

8. MEDICATION

Using a Pill Planner

It is very important to take the correct dosage of medication at the right time, whether it is prescribed for morning, noon or night. The easiest and best way to do this is to use a seven day pill planner.

A seven day pill planner has all the days of the week with separate compartments within that day for the pills that must be taken. Be sure to read the pill bottles carefully to get the exact dose and medication into each day.

I find it works best to fill the planner once a week on the same day of the week so you do not accidently overlap your pills. This way you can also get the task of filling the pill planner into part of your planned weekly schedule.

Write the day of the week you will fill your planner in your Day-Timer®, and this will keep you from forgetting to fill the planner or take your meds and will act as a self-check system to make sure you have taken your medication as scheduled.

Reordering Medication

Filling your pill planner not only acts as an effective tool for taking correct dosages on time, it also allows you to keep track of the amount of medication you have left. This then allows you to determine when your prescription needs to be refilled.

For example, after filling your pill planner with medication #a, #b and #c you find that there is plenty of #a and #b but only a couple of #c. This means it is time to reorder pill #c. Refilling this prescription ahead of running out gives the pharmacy time to fill it before you need it.

All the information you need to know about the medication is on the label on the bottle. This includes the prescription number, the name of the medication, the dosage, the name and number of your pharmacy, your name and the prescribing doctor's name. Call your pharmacy, tell them your name and let them know you would like to refill a prescription. They will ask for the prescription number and the name of the pill or medicine. Ask when you can pick up the medication so you can avoid making extra trips to the store.

Please note, when filling a prescription at the pharmacy for the first time, you must bring the written prescription from your doctor to the pharmacy.

If you have a mail-in option on your insurance to refill your prescription, you must fill out the mail-in form and include the prescription from the doctor. Be sure to check the cost of the prescription and the amount of medicine you will receive. All of this information will be on the order form and will be sent to you from your insurance company.

If you are refilling a mail-in prescription, you just have to phone in your order with the prescription number found on the label of your bottle. The company will then send an invoice with the prescription for you to pay. Be sure to allow enough time when you order so you don't run out of your medicine.

9. WORKING

If you have been head injured and are seeking employment, keep your reasoning and goals realistic. After my surgery I was anxious to return to work, but not to the job I had left. I felt I could and I wanted to do any other job at a higher rate of pay.

However, the results of my testing showed that the best job for me would be the cleaning field or a job that was repetitive. I thought to myself that this could not be as other members of my family were elevator mechanics, business professionals, researchers and lawyers.

I had the desire to become more in life, but now did not seem to have the ability. That created conflict and disbelief within me.

As a result I had further testing which showed the same results as the first tests. Remember, these tests are to clarify the path which you should follow in order to perform a job to the best of your ability. You, in turn, will be a happier person if you take this advice instead of fighting with yourself or focusing on other people's success.

Upon applying for a job, fill out the application and in any section that reads "disabilities or limitations" you should list whatever yours may be so that people involved in hiring or supervision are aware of what assistance or accommodation you might need.

The manager whom I work with on a daily basis is aware of my memory impairment, so he understands that my tasks either have to be in a written form of request or that he has to allow me the time to make a self-notation of it. In this way I can perform and complete the request.

I carry a notepad with me so I can write down the request when I am asked to do something. There is more to making a notation than just writing down something like "mop floor." I write down a list as follows:

1. The date and time
2. The name of the person making the request
3. The time I complete the task

Then I report back to the person who originated the request to let them know that I have completed the job and when it was finished.

I would like to share a work experience that gives an example of some of the topics in this book. I had applied for a position as a cleaner for a company and had been hired. I had worked for the company successfully until I had some complications with my medication.

My main dysfunction was a seizure disorder prior to my surgery in 1988. Due to the later effects of my surgery, I would stare aimlessly at people and objects. This proved to be intimidating even though I meant nothing by it and was not aware I was doing it. It was merely a fixation due to the effect of the head trauma. But it created chaos.

A company within one of the buildings which I cleaned was uncomfortable and wanted me relieved of my duties.

Learning of the discomfort, I chose to readjust my schedule myself, changing the order in which I cleaned the floors so that I no longer had any contact with the people on that floor.

I then immediately contacted my physician to make him aware of what was going on, and to see if there might be any test or medication adjustments that could be made to correct the staring problem.

The outcome of this staring situation was that some friends of the person who complained frequently make sarcastic and snide remarks to or about me, and I sometimes receive the "cold shoulder" from other people within the supervisory positions and co-workers.

I write this to show examples of real-life situations which I have had to face within the recent past. Even in the best job that fits your abilities, things can and will go wrong sometimes, and these can seem to make your situation or workplace chaotic.

Don't get discouraged when you run into these kinds of people or have problems. Turn to the proper channels such as your immediate work supervisor or group person to help you solve the issue at hand. Then just go about your job functions as you did before.

10. SOCIALIZING

Socializing is somewhat difficult for me due to the fact that I work 12 hours a day, Monday-Friday, and have a severe memory deficit. It takes another whole strategy in order to socialize, only one factor being to find the time. However, it is important to allow yourself time to go out if for no other reason than just to unwind or have dinner.

One of the key things I do when I go out is to try to go to familiar places. If I am in a new place, I get seated as close to the entrance that I came in so that I can remember which way to exit and be closest to my car.

Generally Speaking

A situation that happens often and makes all persons involved feel uncomfortable involves meeting and greeting new people, especially if they are in a group. It could be impossible to remember all of the names of those you have just met without feeling foolish.

Starting the conversation with just "Hi" or "What's up?" can get the conversation going and allow you to say hello to many people at one time without having to specifically identify any one person by name.

Later, use memory techniques such as "Bob has brown hair" or "Mary has on a red dress." This is a technique called association and can help you to remember who people are.

Start a conversation off with a topic like the weather or what happened over the weekend. After getting to know the person a little better, you can work into the conversation information about your impairment, but remember to be selective about whom you share this information with. It is your personal business. I have found that if you choose to share this information too soon or with people you might see every day, some of them may tend to shy away from association of you, so be selective about whom you trust.

11. IN CONCLUSION

Losing Sight of Systems

Systems, even the ones I am writing about, work better for some people than others. Choose the one that you can best understand and develop into an everyday practice. Choose one that allows you to perform tasks accurately and with the most ease.

Do not let anyone tell you there is only one right way to do a task: there may be a couple of different ways to get them done. Pick the one that allows you to get the task done correctly in a way that you will understand.

Even with the best system, things can happen that can cause you to miscalculate and cause things to malfunction. Don't panic. Retrace your steps in your system back to a point you have already completed successfully. You should then be able to figure out what caused the breakdown. Correct it and go on!

Using these ideas should help enable you to be more self-sufficient in everyday life. These tips have helped me reduce the chaos of everyday living to allow me to successfully complete the tasks I needed to complete. I hope they help you too.

APPENDIX

Tools

a) Day-Timer® Page
b) Deposit and Withdrawal Slips
c) Bill Paying Checklist
d) Grocery List

DayTimer® Page

Below is an example of what a DayTimer® or other calendar page may look like. These pages are helpful for scheduling activities and tracking money in your wallet. The example shows how items may be recorded.

Friday, June 23			Friday, June 23	
Appointments			**Notes**	
8				
9				
	9:45 am, Jiffy Lube, Burlington			
10			Go to Post Office and mail bills ✓	
11				
12				
1				
2				
3				
4				
5				
6				
7				
8				
Todays To do List				
$10.00 Gas				
$18.00 Food Shopping		BB: $40.00		
$28.00 DT		DT: -$28.00		
		$12.00		

Deposit and Withdrawal Slips

Below are examples of Deposit and Withdrawal slips that you may find at your bank. The examples have been filled out with typical information. Withdrawal slips found at the bank are often a different color than the deposit slips.

If you are using your own deposit slip (from your checking account, for example), some of the information, like your name and the account number, will already be printed for you.

City Bank		Deposit Amount	
Deposit Slip		Checks 1	100.00
		2	50.00
Date	11/22/2009		
Name	Charlie Jones	Cash	30.00
Account #	01-234-56789	Total	180.00

City Bank		Withdrawal Amount	
Withdrawal Slip			
		Cash	30.00
Date	11/22/2009		
Name	Charlie Jones		
Signature	*Charlie Jones*		
Account #	01-234-56789		

Bill Paying Checklist

The bill paying checklist will help you organize your bills and make sure that you don't miss any payments. You should fill the sheet in with each of your bills as described in section 4.

Month: **Year:**

Bill Name	Amount Due	Due Date	Amount Paid	Date Paid	Check Number	Notes
Mortgage						
Car Payment						
Insurance (House)						
Insurance (Car)						
Electric						
Oil						
Telephone						
Credit Card 1						
Credit Card 2						
Food						
Gas						
Other						
Quarterly/Annual Payments						
Town Water/Sewer						
Excise Tax						
Other						
Total Payments						

Voided Checks Number	Date	Amount	Notes

Grocery List

The grocery list shown below is an example of how the list would be set up for a typical grocery store. This is only a partial list. You would want to create a similar list for the grocery store that you use. For each aisle, record the food you typically buy from that aisle. Instructions for using the list can be found in section 5.

Market Basket Grocery List

Dairy
2% milk (1/2 gallon)
Lactaid milk 100 (red)
O.J. - Chaquita pinapple/orange/banana
Butter - Land O' Lakes
Sharp cheddar cheese
Philadelphia cream cheese
Creamer (1 quart half & half)

Aisle 1
Bread crumbs
Frozen prepared meat, turkey
Stuffing

Aisle 2
Cooking oil
Croutons
Mayonnaise - Cains (small jar)
Pickles
Mustard
Salad dressing - blue cheese, italian

Aisle 3
Cereals - Cocoa puffs, Life
Hot cereals - oatmeal
Pop tarts

Aisle 4
Barbeque sauce
Beans
Canned meats
Grated cheese
Ketchup
Macaroni/noodles
Sauce - Prego tomato
Soy sauce
Tuna fish

Aisle 5
Candy - Silver mints (1 bag)
Fruit snacks - Strawberry gushers
Jelly
Pancake mix
Peanut butter
Raisins
Syrup

Aisle 6
Aspirin - Advil
Cold remedies
Conditioner/Shampoo - Pantene Pro V
Deoderant
Gel
Soap - Dove (2 pink bars)

Aisle 7
Brooms
Kleenex
Napkins
Paper towels

Meat
Chicken
Hamburger
Roast beef
Steak

Frozen section
Bagels - Lernders egg (1 package0
Ice cream - Hendries chocolate
Frozen crinkle fries
Frozen waffles - Eggo

Produce
Bananas
Carrots
Lettuce - iceburg

Circle around item = buy item
Check next to item = you've already picked out item and out in carriage